SPORTS HEROES

SIMONE BILES

Hi, pleased to meet you.

We hope you enjoy our book about *Simone Biles!*

WELBECK
CHILDREN'S BOOKS

SIMON and DAN

Published in the USA in 2024 by Welbeck Children's Books
An imprint of Hachette Children's Group
Part of Hodder & Stoughton Limited
Carmelite House, 50 Victoria Embankment
London EC4Y 0DZ
An Hachette UK Company
www.hachette.co.uk
www.hachettechildrens.co.uk
Text © 2024 Simon Mugford
Design & Illustration © 2024 Dan Green
ISBN: 978-1-80453-669-8

Writer: Simon Mugford
Designer and Illustrator: Dan Green
Design Manager: Sam James
Senior Commissioning Editor: Suhel Ahmed
Production: Melanie Robertson

Printed in the UK
10 9 8 7 6 5 4 3 2 1

Statistics and records correct as of March 2024.

SPORTS HEROES

SIMONE BILES

SIMON MUGFORD **DAN GREEN**

CONTENTS

CHAPTER 1 - **HIGH FLIER**..**5**

CHAPTER 2 - **LITTLE SIMONE**...**13**

CHAPTER 3 - **JUNIOR TO SENIOR**.......................................**23**

CHAPTER 4 - **FANTASTIC GYMNASTICS**.......................**33**

CHAPTER 5 - **WORLD CHAMPION**.......................................**47**

CHAPTER 6 - **GYMNASTICS LEGENDS**.........................**61**

CHAPTER 7 - **GOLDEN GIRL**..**71**

CHAPTER 8 - **RECORD BREAKER**.......................................**81**

CHAPTER 9 - **THE BILES SKILLS**...**91**

CHAPTER 10 - **HIGHS AND LOWS**.....................................**105**

CHAPTER 11 - **AMERICAN ICON**...**113**

HI SIMONE!

SIMONE BILES is an **American sports icon.** Since growing up in foster care, Simone has gone on to overcome personal and professional challenges to win medal after medal in gymnastics and become a . . .

GLOBAL SUPERSTAR!

This book is all about her!

6

WHAT MAKES *SIMONE* SUCH AN *INCREDIBLE* GYMNAST?

GIFTED

Some people are born with natural talent and Simone is overflowing with it!

POWER

Simone is small, but mighty! Her physical strength and muscular power set her apart from her rivals.

DEDICATION
Training for hours on end, every day since she was a little girl, Simone has dedicated her life to the sport.

SUPPORT
Being surrounded by a supportive family, team, and coaching staff has helped Simone achieve her goals.

RESILIENCE
Simone has shown awesome levels of toughness to overcome the hard times in her personal and professional life.

SIMONE IN *NUMBERS*

Simone's gymnastics career has earned her some *VERY IMPRESSIVE* numbers . . .

30
WORLD CHAMPIONSHIP MEDALS

23 GOLD

4 SILVER

3 BRONZE

No gymnast has won more *World Championship* medals than Simone.

7 OLYMPIC MEDALS

4 GOLD

1 SILVER

2 BRONZE

5 SPECIAL GYMNASTIC MOVES NAMED AFTER HER

Estimated

$16 MILLION FORTUNE

7 MILLION

followers on Instagram

SIMONE BILES I.D.

NAME: Simone Arianne Biles Owens

DATE OF BIRTH: March 14, 1997

PLACE OF BIRTH: Columbus, Ohio

NATIONALITY: American

HEIGHT: 4 feet 8 inches (1.42 m)

GYMNASTIC DISCIPLINES: Floor exercise, balance beam, vault, uneven bars

CHAPTER 2

LITTLE SIMONE

Simone Biles was born in **Columbus,**

in the State of Ohio, in 1997.

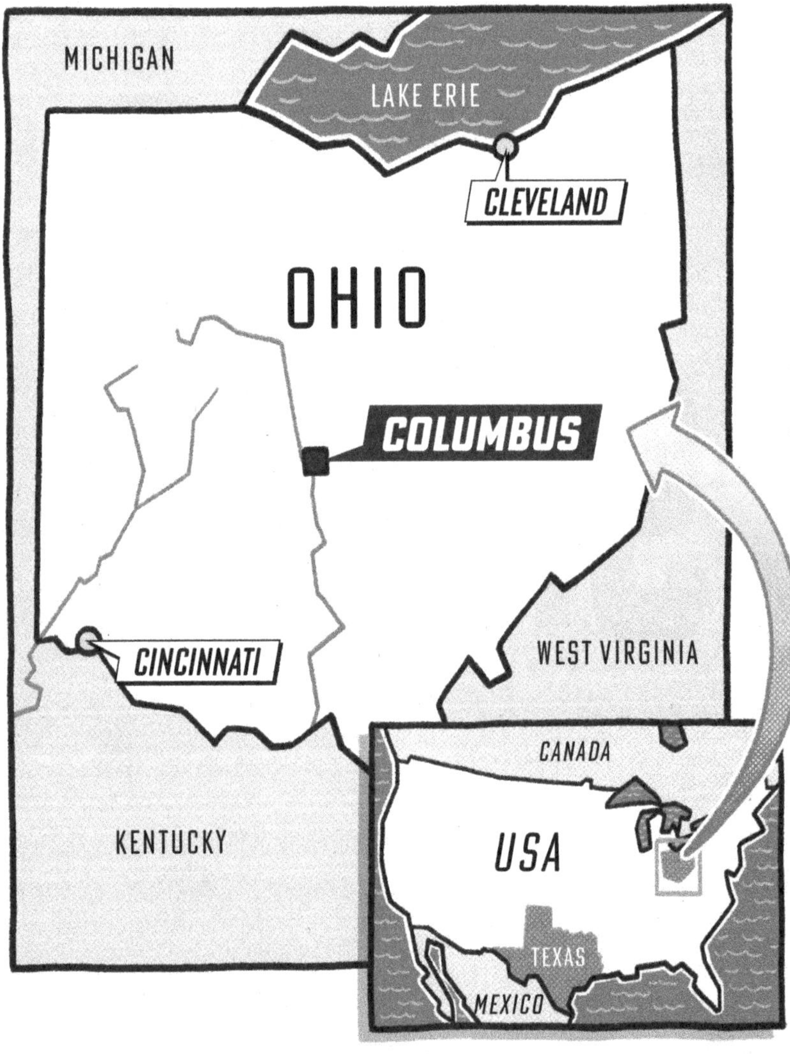

MICHIGAN

LAKE ERIE

CLEVELAND

OHIO

COLUMBUS

CINCINNATI

WEST VIRGINIA

KENTUCKY

CANADA

USA

TEXAS

MEXICO

She lived with her mom **Shannon** . . .

older sister **Ashley** . . .

older brother **Tevin** . . .

and her younger sister **Adria.**

Life at home was **very difficult** for Simone's family. Her mom had struggled with addiction and her father had left the family home.

When Simone was three, she went into *foster care* with her brother and sisters.

The family split up when **Ashley** and **Tevin** were adopted by their **great aunt.**

Simone and her younger sister Adria were adopted by their grandfather **Ron Biles** and his wife **Nellie.**

Simone was **six years old** when she and her sister went to live with Ron and Nellie.

They lived in **Spring,** near **Houston** in Texas.

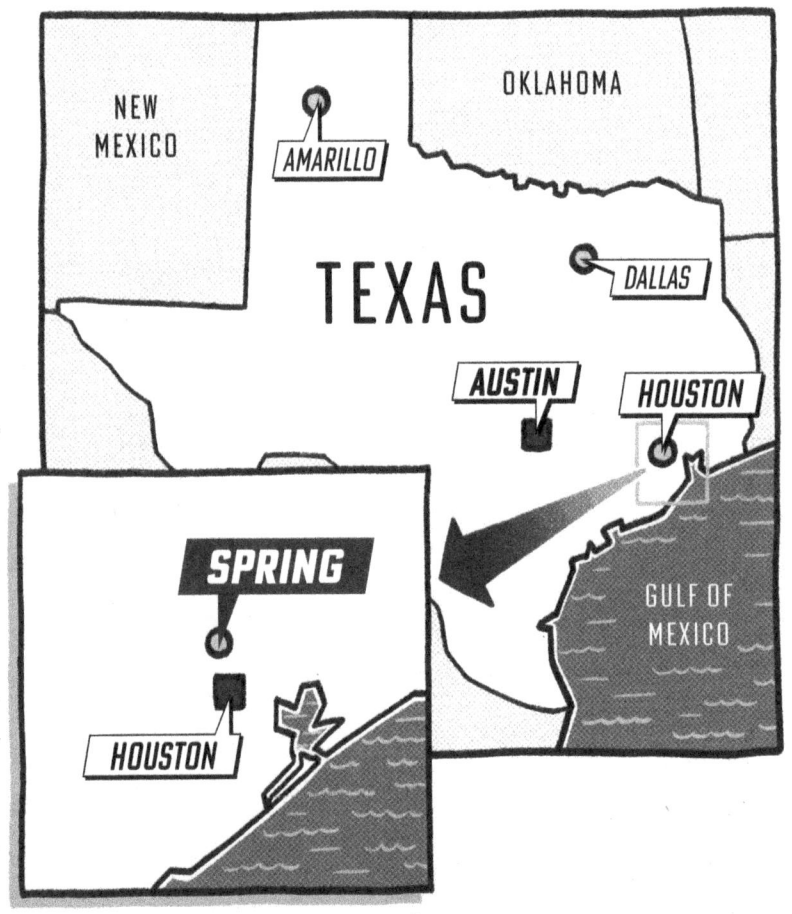

Simone and Adria lived in a **happy, safe home** that was full of **love** and **support**.

> Best of all, for Simone, they had a *trampoline!*

And she bounced . . . and jumped . . . and flipped on it for hours on end.

BOING!

One day, shortly after she moved to Texas, Simone went on a field trip to a **gymnastics center.**

She watched the **gymnasts bouncing, jumping,** and **flipping.**

I CAN DO THAT . . .

20

And she tried it herself.

One of the coaches told Simone she had a **real talent** and that she should try doing gymnastics . . .

"I DIDN'T THINK IN THAT MOMENT MY LIFE WOULD HAVE CHANGED AND I WOULD BE WHO I AM TODAY."

Simone Biles

22

CHAPTER 3

JUNIOR TO SENIOR

Ron and Nellie signed Simone and her sister Adria up to the **Bannon's Gymnastix** club in **Houston.**

At Bannon's, Simone soon proved that she was **born to be a gymnast.**

The little girl in a **sparkly leotard** worked harder than anyone else at the club.

Simone would **jump, bounce,** and **spin faster, higher,** and **harder** than even the older girls.

Aimee Boorman was the Head Coach at Bannon's Gymnastix. Aimee recognized Simone's star potential and began coaching her in **2005** when Simone was **eight years old.**

Simone worked with Aimee **every day after school,** quickly working her way up through the different levels of gymnastics.

Simone's **relentless energy** was fantastic for the gym, but not so helpful for school.

She found it hard to concentrate and was diagnosed with a condition known as **ADHD** (attention deficit hyperactivity disorder).

Simone was given some **medicine** to help her **focus.** It helped her with schoolwork.

Simone turned **14** in **2011,** which was an important year in her ambition to conquer gynmastics. She had reached the highest levels as a regular gymnast—now was the time to become an **elite junior.**

As an **elite gymnast,** Simone would dedicate her life to the sport, taking part in the biggest events and competing for the **U.S. national team**.

She left school to be **homeschooled** so

that she could spend up to **eight hours a day** in training.

SIMONE'S JUNIOR RECORD

YEAR	COMPETITION	ALL-AROUND	VAULT	UNEVEN BARS	BALANCE BEAM	FLOOR
2011	American Classic	BRONZE	GOLD	8th	GOLD	4th
	U.S. Classic	20th	5th	34th	11th	5th
	U.S. National Championships	14th	7th	22nd	10th	12th
2012	U.S. Classic	GOLD	GOLD	10th	6th	SILVER
	U.S. National Championships	BRONZE	GOLD	6th	6th	6th

At **15,** Simone was too young to compete in the **2012 Summer Olympics** in London.

But as she watched the tournament on TV and saw the U.S. team win medals, she dreamed that one day she would represent her country and become an **Olympic Champion.**

Simone remained **focused**, training hard
and competing as she prepared to make the
step up to a **senior elite** gymnast.

"I MADE A LOT OF SACRIFICES. I DECIDED TO . . . GO TO HOME SCHOOL. I GAVE UP ALL THE SCHOOL DANCES. I'VE NEVER BEEN TO A PROM. BUT I FELL IN LOVE WITH THE SPORT."

Simone Biles

CHAPTER 4

FANTASTIC GYMNASTICS

ANCIENT GYMNASTICS

Gymnastics originated in **ancient Greece about 2,500 years ago.** Back then, only men competed in sports, such as . . .

running . . .

floor exercises . . .

MODERN *GYMNASTICS*

Gymnastics, as we know it today, began in **Europe** in the early **nineteenth century.**

A teacher with a long name, **Johann Christoph Friedrich Guts-Muths,** introduced gymnastics to schools in Germany as a way of "improving the body and mind."

Oof!

Meanwhile, in nearby **Prussia, Friedrich Ludwig Jahn** promoted gymnastics as a way of preparing young men for the army. They used equipment similar to that used today.

Gymnastics featured at the first **"Modern Olympics"** in **Athens** in **1896.** But it was **only for men.**

Women gymnasts first competed at the Olympics in *1928.*

SIMONE'S EVENTS:

FLOOR EXERCISE

The **floor exercise** is held on a carpeted, slightly sprung floor that measures 39 feet by 39 feet (12m x 12m).

Women gymnasts perform a **routine set to music** that lasts **90 seconds,** and it can include jumps, dances, acrobatics, and up to four **tumbling passes.**

This is the event where gymnasts have the **freedom** to really express themselves.

The floor exercise is Simone's *favorite event.* She holds the record for most titles (seven altogether) in this event.

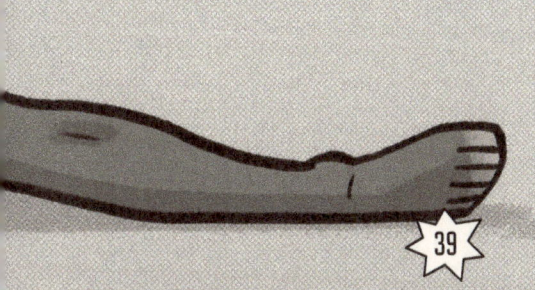

VAULT

In the **vault,** the gymnast runs down a runway, jumps onto a springboard, and leaps—hands first—toward the vault.

They propel themselves off the vault and perform spectacular **twists** and **somersaults** before landing on the other side of the vault.

Simone has won *three* vault titles.

BALANCE BEAM

The **balance beam** is a padded, sprung, narrow beam on which the gymnasts perform acrobatics made up of **steps, jumps, leaps, turns,** and **posed positions** in a routine that lasts between 70 and 90 seconds.

Only women perform the balance beam competitively.

Simone has won *four World titles* on the balance beam—a record.

SIMONE'S EVENTS:
UNEVEN BARS

The **uneven bars** are two horizontal bars set side by side but at different heights. The gymnasts **swing, leap,** and **spin** between the two bars.

This is Simone's most challenging event— her height puts her at a disadvantage.

ALL-AROUND

In the **all-around** event, gymnasts compete in all four artistic disciplines. Simone is a **six-time world champion** in the all-around.

"I WOULD HOPE I WOULD INSPIRE KIDS EVERYWHERE TO KNOW THAT YOU CAN DO ANYTHING YOU PUT YOUR MIND TO."

Simone Biles

CHAPTER 5

WORLD CHAMPION

Simone's **senior gymnastics** career began in 2013. She competed in tournaments at home and abroad, showing off her talents and winning medals.

But at the **U.S. Classic,** Simone performed poorly and picked up an injury. It could have really dented the confidence of the young athlete and affected her future in the sport.

But with the support of her coach and a **sports psychologist,** Simone learned to focus and enjoy herself—and her sport—again.

And she's not looked back since . . .

Just a few short weeks after her **disastrous U.S. Classic,** Simone competed at the **U.S. National Championships.**

She won **gold** in the **all-around** and **silver** in the four individual events.

Simone was later named in the senior national team—she was heading to the **World Artistic Gymnastics Championships!**

WHOOP!

The World Artistic Gymnastics Championships was first held in 1903 and is hosted in different cities around the world.

2013 WORLD ARTISTIC GYMNASTICS CHAMPIONSHIPS

ANTWERP, BELGIUM

SEPTEMBER 30–OCTOBER 6, 2013

Simone qualified for all the events, including a **first-place qualification** for the all-around.

Simone went on to win **GOLD** in the **all-around** and **GOLD** in the **floor exercise**.

The little girl from Ohio who'd had a difficult start in life was now a . . .

DOUBLE WORLD CHAMPION!

She also won *silver* on the *vault* and *bronze* on the *balance beam*.

GROUNDBREAKING

At her first **World Championships,**

16-year-old Simone had become . . .

THE FIRST **AMERICAN GYMNAST** TO QUALIFY FOR ALL THE EVENTS SINCE **SHANNON MILLER** IN **1991**

Shannon
Miller

THE FIRST **AFRICAN AMERICAN PERSON** EVER TO WIN THE ALL-AROUND

She was also **breaking barriers** with her performance—her **jumps, moves,** and **speed** were all way ahead of her rivals.

Simone even performed a move in the **floor exercise** that had never been done before—now known as the "Biles" *(see page 94).*

2014 WORLD ARTISTIC GYMNASTICS CHAMPIONSHIPS

NANNING, CHINA

OCTOBER 3-12, 2014

Simone was the standout performer in the competition, qualifying in first place for all the events except the uneven bars.

This time, she picked up **FOUR GOLD MEDALS,** for the all-around, balance beam, floor exercise, and the team event.

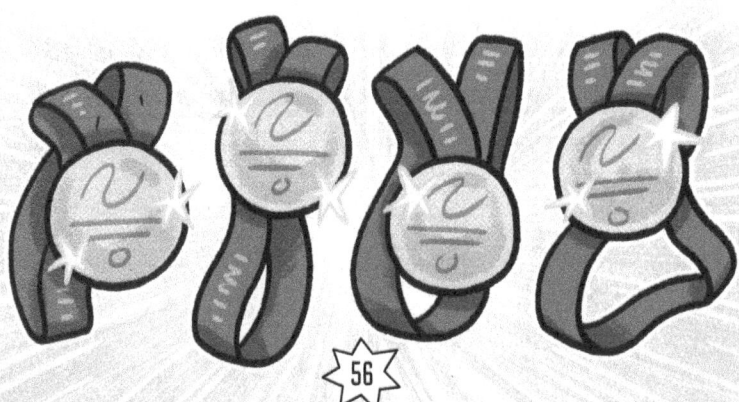

Simone became the **first American gymnast** to retain the all-around title since **Shannon Miller** 20 years previously.

Simone had now **won more** World Championship gold medals (six) than any other American gymnast.

2015 WORLD ARTISTIC GYMNASTICS CHAMPIONSHIPS

GLASGOW, UNITED KINGDOM

OCTOBER 23–NOVEMBER 1, 2015

In this, her third **World Championships,** Simone would continue her record-breaking rise to gymnastics superstardom.

Despite a poor performance (by Simone's standards) in the all-around, she still won **gold,** becoming the **first-ever woman** to win three back-to-back all-around titles!

She also picked up **gold** in the balance beam, floor exercise, and team event.

Simone had now won **10 World Championship** gold medals—more than any other woman gymnast.

And she was still only *18!*

"WHEN I FIRST SAW HER, I WAS LIKE, 'WOW, THIS KID HAS SOMETHING.' BUT WHAT IT WAS AND HOW FAR SHE COULD GO WITH IT, I HAD NO IDEA."

Aimee Boorman, Simone's coach

CHAPTER 6

GYMNASTICS LEGENDS

LARISA **LATYNINA**

NATIONALITY: RUSSIAN (SOVIET)

OLYMPIC RECORD: 9 x GOLD, 5 x SILVER, 4 x BRONZE

WORLD CHAMPS RECORD: 9 x GOLD, 4 x SILVER, 1 x BRONZE

A former dancer, Larisa made her debut at the **1954 World Championships** in Rome, but it was at the **1956 Melbourne Olympics** where she made her name. There, she won the first four of her **nine Olympic gold medals,** a record for any gymnast, male or female. Larisa's dominance of the sport helped establish the Soviet Union as a world force in gymnastics in the 1950s and 60s.

VERA CASLAVSKA

NATIONALITY: CZECHOSLOVAKIAN (CZECH)

OLYMPIC RECORD: 7 x GOLD, 4 x SILVER

WORLD CHAMPS RECORD: 4 x GOLD, 5 x SILVER, 1 x BRONZE

Vera began her sporting career as a **figure skater** but switched to gymnastics, debuting at the **1958 World Championships** in Moscow. She won **22 international titles** between 1959 and 1968, including **seven Olympic golds.** Vera is the only gymnast, male or female, to win gold in each gymnastics event at the Olympics.

NASTIA LIUKIN

NATIONALITY: AMERICAN (BORN IN RUSSIA)

OLYMPIC RECORD: 1 x GOLD, 3 x SILVER, 1 x BRONZE

WORLD CHAMPS RECORD: 4 x GOLD, 5 x SILVER

The daughter of former Soviet gymnasts Valeri Liukin and Anna Kotchneva, Nastia starred for **Team USA** at the **2008 Beijing Olympics,** where she won **five medals,** including gold in the all-around. She has dedicated herself to the sport, hosting the annual **Nastia Liukin Cup** competition in the USA.

GINA GOGEAN

NATIONALITY: ROMANIAN

OLYMPIC RECORD: 2 x SILVER, 3 x BRONZE

WORLD CHAMPS RECORD: 9 x GOLD, 2 x SILVER, 4 x BRONZE

One of the **most decorated gymnasts** of all time, Gina was famous for her consistency and longevity in a dominant period throughout the 1990s. While younger gymnasts were attempting fancier tricks, Gina stuck to what she knew and she did it brilliantly, picking up **15 World Championship** and **five Olympic** medals.

SVETLANA **KHORKINA**

NATIONALITY: RUSSIAN (SOVIET)

OLYMPIC RECORD: 2 x GOLD, 4 x SILVER 1, x BRONZE

WORLD CHAMPS RECORD: 9 x GOLD, 8 x SILVER, 3 x BRONZE

Svetlana was known as the **"Queen of the Bars,"** where her height gave her an unmatched advantage in the uneven bars. She won **five World Championship** and **two Olympic gold** medals in that event. She was also the first gymnast to win **three all-around golds** in the World Championships.

NADIA COMANECI

NATIONALITY: ROMANIAN

OLYMPIC RECORD: 5 x GOLD, 3 x SILVER, 1 x BRONZE

WORLD CHAMPS RECORD: 2 x GOLD, 2 x SILVER

At the **1976 Olympics** in Montreal, Nadia was catapulted into international superstardom when she became the first gymnast to score a **perfect 10.0 points** in the Games. Incredibly, she was just **14 years old.** Another six perfect scores helped her win three golds at those Games. A true **gymnastics legend,** Nadia helped popularize the sport during the 1970s.

MARY LOU RETTON

NATIONALITY: AMERICAN

OLYMPIC RECORD: 1 x GOLD, 2 x SILVER, 2 x BRONZE

WORLD CHAMPS RECORD: NONE

Mary Lou became a global star at the **1984 Los Angeles Olympics,** where she became the **first American woman** to win Olympic gold in the all-around event, a record she held for 20 years. She was a hugely popular figure in 1980s sports, earning the nickname, **"America's Sweetheart."**

OLGA KORBUT

NATIONALITY: BELARUSIAN (SOVIET)

OLYMPIC RECORD: 4 x GOLD, 2 x SILVER

WORLD CHAMPS RECORD: 2 x GOLD, 4 x SILVER

At the age of 17, Olga's performance at the **1972 Munich Olympics** revolutionized gymnastics. Previously, the sport focused on ballet-style elegance, but Olga introduced **spectacular acrobatics,** making gymnastics wildly popular. Her influence and legacy is immense, with the *"Korbut Flip"* being a key move on the balance beam to this day.

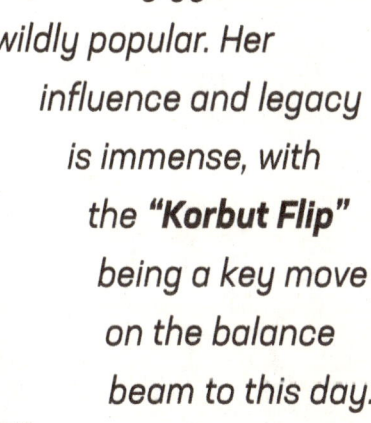

SHANNON MILLER

NATIONALITY: AMERICAN

OLYMPIC RECORD: 2 x GOLD, 2 x SILVER, 3 x BRONZE

WORLD CHAMPS RECORD: 5 x GOLD, 3 x SILVER, 1 x BRONZE

Shannon's record of **nine WC** and **seven Olympic medals** makes her the second-most-decorated American gymnast of all time—only **Simone Biles** has more. Shannon was part of the record-breaking **"Magnificent Seven"** U.S. women's team at the **1996 Atlanta Olympics** and her achievements have proved an inspiration for Simone.

CHAPTER 7

GOLDEN GIRL

Simone kicked off the **2016 season** competing in the **Pacific Rim Championships**, the **U.S. Classic**, and the **U.S. National Championships**, collecting **seven gold medals** along the way.

Simone won another **three golds** at the trials for that summer's Olympic Games.

She was selected for the USA team, and set off to **Rio de Janeiro** in **Brazil** to compete in her first-ever **Olympics!**

Simone was one of **five** members of the U.S.

Gymnastics team. They called themselves . . .

THE FINAL FIVE

Simone Biles

Gabby Douglas

Laurie Hernandez

Madison Kocian

Aly Raisman

And Simone's long-term coach **Aimee Boorman** was in charge of the team.

Simone led the **Final Five** to win **gold**

in the **team event** . . .

She won another

gold in the

all-around . . .

Then it was **gold**

again for Simone

on the **vault** . . .

On the **balance beam,** she had a wobble– but still managed to win **bronze . . .**

And then, in the **floor exercise,** Simone's favorite discipline, she performed a routine to a Brazilian samba soundtrack that stunned the crowd– somersaulting and leaping in her sparking leotard to win her **fourth Olympic gold!**

SHE WAS SENSATIONAL!

The Final Five won a **U.S. gymnastics team record** of **nine medals** overall—the most for any team since the **Soviet Union** at the **1972 Games.**

Simone's four Olympic gold medals are the **most for any American gymnast** at a single Games.

Simone was America's star athlete—and she proudly carried the **Stars and Stripes** at the Olympic closing ceremony.

After the Olympics, the medical records of Simone and some Team USA athletes were leaked by **computer hackers.** It showed that she been using medicine for her ADHD.

Some people said she should have her medals taken away . . .

But she defended herself and **spoke up for millions of young people** who have the same condition.

*HAVING **ADHD** IS NOTHING TO BE ASHAMED OF.*

CHAPTER 8

RECORD BREAKER

TAKING A BREAK

In 2017, Simone decided to **take a break** from gymnastics. She had been training and competing nonstop for **13 years.** She needed a rest!

Simone **wrote a book** about her life so far . . .

She did some **charity work** and **visited schools** . . .

And she even appeared on the TV show *Dancing with the Stars!*

After more than year out, Simone returned to gymnastics in **2018.** Coach Aimee had moved to Florida to be with her family, so Simone teamed up with a new coach, **Laurent Landi.**

HI!

And she returned in some style, winning five gold medals at the **U.S. National Championships** and bringing home a medal in **every single event** at the **2018 World Championships** in Doha, Qatar.

SIMONE'S 2018 RECORD

COMPETITION	TEAM	ALL-AROUND	VAULT	UNEVEN BARS	BALANCE BEAM	FLOOR EXERCISE
U.S. Classic	–	GOLD	–	10th	GOLD	GOLD
U.S. National Championships	–	GOLD	GOLD	GOLD	GOLD	GOLD
Worlds Team Selection Camp	–	GOLD	GOLD	SILVER	4th	GOLD
World Championships	GOLD	GOLD	GOLD	SILVER	BRONZE	GOLD

In **2019,** Simone was in awesome form, picking up medals and performing moves that had never been seen before in competitions.

At the U.S. National Championships, she performed a **triple-twisting double somersault** in the **floor exercise**–the first woman ever to do it . . .

And Simone followed that with the first-ever **double twisting double somersault** off the balance beam–

INCREDIBLE!

SIMONE'S 2019 RECORD

COMPETITION	TEAM	ALL-AROUND	VAULT	UNEVEN BARS	BALANCE BEAM	FLOOR EXERCISE
Stuttgart World Cup	-	GOLD	-	-	-	-
U.S. Classic	-	GOLD	-	5th	BRONZE	GOLD
U.S. National Championships	-	GOLD	GOLD	BRONZE	GOLD	GOLD
Worlds Team Selection Camp	GOLD	GOLD	4th	SILVER	GOLD	-
World Championships	GOLD	GOLD	GOLD	5th	GOLD	GOLD

RECORD BREAKER

Since returning to the sport in 2018, Simone has set so many new records. She is now . . .

THE FIRST WOMAN TO WIN **FOUR ALL-AROUND** WORLD TITLES

WINNER OF **MOST WORLD CHAMPIONSHIP GOLD MEDALS** (23) OF ANY GYMNAST, MALE OR FEMALE

THE **FIRST AMERICAN** TO WIN A **WORLD CHAMPIONSHIP MEDAL** IN EVERY EVENT

JOINT RECORD HOLDER FOR THE **MOST GOLD MEDALS** (5) AT A SINGLE WORLD CHAMPIONSHIPS

This was the first time since *1958*.

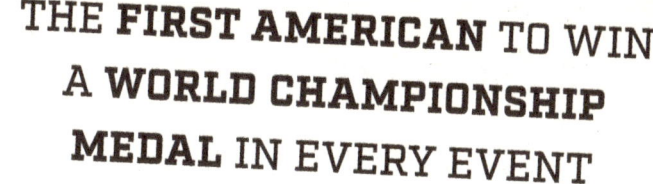

WINNER OF MORE **WORLD CHAMPIONSHIP MEDALS** (30) THAN ANY OTHER GYMNAST IN HISTORY, MALE OR FEMALE.

"WHEN YOU'VE HAD SO MUCH SUCCESS IN THE SPORT, WHAT BRINGS YOU BACK IN THE GYM IS SOMETHING ORIGINAL, DIFFERENT STUFF. IT'S NOT JUST WINNING."

Simone's coach, Laurent Landi

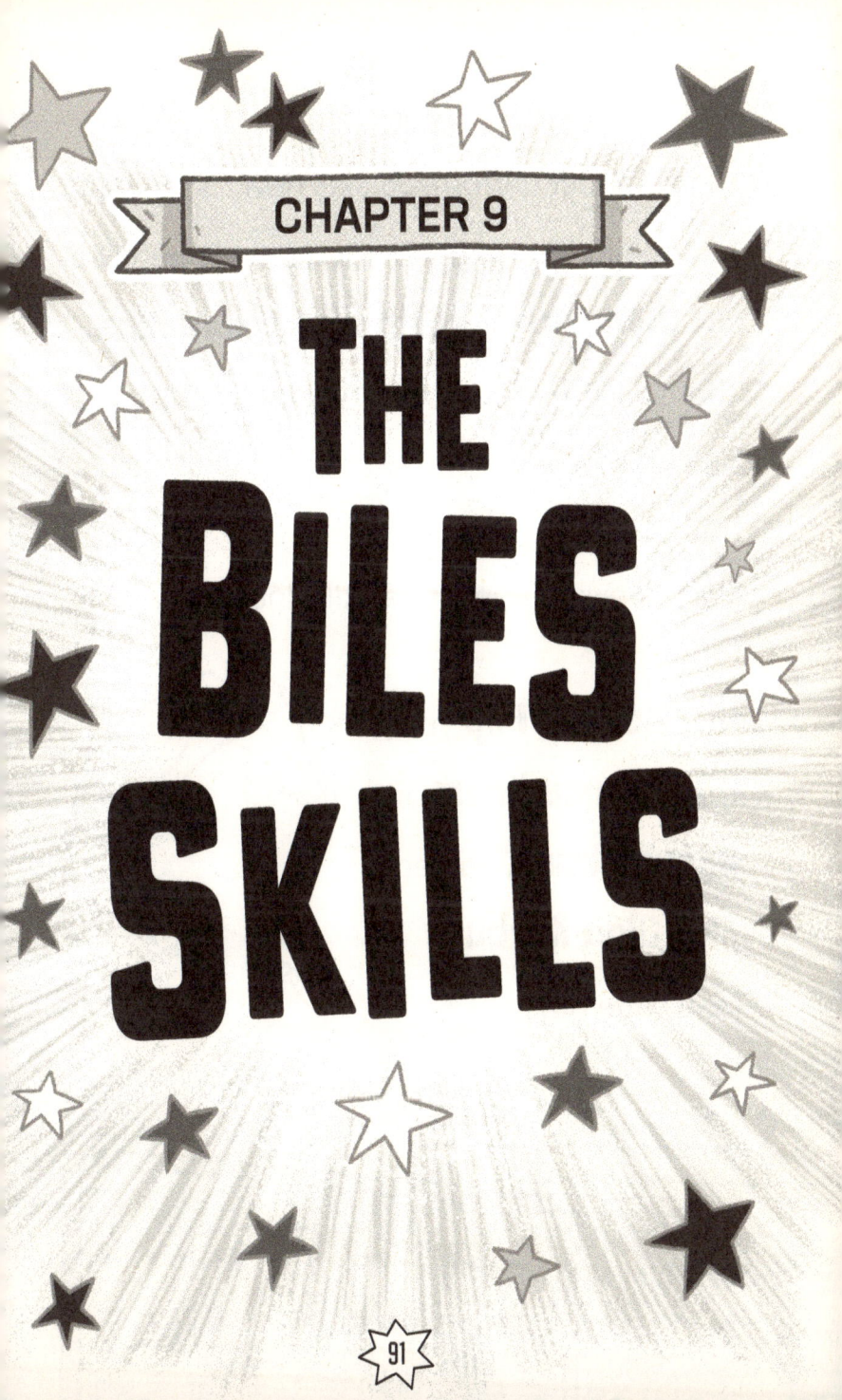

CHAPTER 9

THE BILES SKILLS

If a gymnast performs a skill never seen before at a major international tournament, such as the **Olympics** or **World Championships,** that skill not only stuns the crowd but is sometimes named after them.

Well-known gymnastics skills include . . .

the **"Korbut Flip"** on the **balance beam** and **uneven bars,** named after **Olga Korbut** *(see page 69)* . . .

and the **"Yurchenko,"** which is a complete move on the vault named after **Natalia Yurchenko.**

Simone Biles has **FIVE** **skills** named after her . . .

FLOOR EXERCISE:

THE "BILES"

This skill is a **double layout with half twist,** which Simone first performed at the **2013 World Championships.**

Simone **flips twice in the air,** with her body out straight (the double layout). Then she does a **half twist** before landing.

The "Biles" has since been performed by **Trinity Thomas** at the **2019 U.S. Nationals** and **Hillary Heron** at the **2023 World Championships.**

FLOOR EXERCISE:

THE "BILES II"

Simone first performed this **double backflip with triple twist** at the **2019 World Championships.**

With **incredible power,** Simone **flips backward twice** in the air and does **three twists** at the same time!

BALANCE BEAM:

THE "BILES"

Simone performed this **double-twisting, double backflip dismount** on the **balance beam** at the **2019 World Championships.**

The skill—**flipping twice while twisting at the same time**—made everyone gasp in disbelief. The judges thought it was **so dangerous** that they gave it a lower rating (worth fewer points) to discourage other gymnasts from trying it.

Simone was not happy!

GRR!

VAULT:

THE "BILES"

Simone debuted this **Yurchenko half-on with two twists** on the **vault** at the **2018 World Championships.**

She starts with a **Yurchenko**—a round-off (a type of cartwheel) into a back handspring onto the vault. Then she performs an awesome, flying **half-turn** and two twists before landing.

It's an *incredible skill*, with Simone the only female to have performed it.

THE "BILES II"

Simone demonstrated this skill—a **Yurchenko double pike vault**—in preparation for the **2020 Tokyo Olympics.** It was named on her return to international competition at the **2023 World Championships.**

Her **Yurchenko,** which finishes with **two backward double flips,** is the hardest

possible move on the vault . . .

"IT WAS JUST SO AMAZING. I WAS AMAZED THAT WE HAVE SIMONE BILES, WHO CAN RAISE US ALL TO THAT KIND OF LEVEL."

Natalia Yurchenko

CHAPTER 10

HIGHS
AND
LOWS

The **2020 Tokyo Olympic Games** took place in **2021,** because of the **Covid pandemic.**

In the competition, something **was not right** with Simone. She was way off her best and she **withdrew** from all the events except the **balance beam.**

Simone won **bronze** in the **balance beam** and the **silver team medal.**

Since 2013, she had been unbeaten in **every team, all-around,** and **floor competition.**

So, what had happened to Simone?

Being an elite-level athlete is extremely demanding, **physically** and **mentally.**

At the **Tokyo Olympics,** Simone experienced the **"twisties"** –a kind of mental block that stops gymnasts from performing twisting moves.

She had withdrawn because she could not compete safely and was **mentally exhausted.**

From then on, Simone focused on her own **well-being,** spoke out about **mental health** in sport, and **supported other athletes** who had similar experiences.

Simone soon put the **Tokyo Olympics** behind her and returned to compete in **2023.**

At the **World Championships in Antwerp,** Simone was back to her **record-breaking** best, winning another **four gold medals.**

She now had a total of **30 World Championship medals**–more than **any gymnast in history,** male or female.

SIMONE'S 2023 RECORD

COMPETITION	TEAM	ALL-AROUND	VAULT	UNEVEN BARS	BALANCE BEAM	FLOOR EXERCISE
U.S. Classic	-	GOLD	-	BRONZE	GOLD	GOLD
U.S. National Championships	-	GOLD	-	BRONZE	GOLD	GOLD
Worlds Team Selection Camp	-	GOLD	-	13th	BRONZE	GOLD
World Championships	GOLD	GOLD	SILVER	5th	GOLD	GOLD

"IT'S OKAY NOT TO BE OKAY. IF YOU DON'T DO WHAT IS RIGHT FOR YOU, THEN YOU'RE NOT GOING TO ENJOY YOUR SPORT."

Simone Biles

CHAPTER 11

AMERICAN ICON

Simone is an **American sports celebrity** and one of the most famous athletes in the world.

In 2021, her **superstar status** was confirmed when she appeared on the cover of *TIME* **Magazine.**

TIME

SIMONE BILES

Gymnastics does not pay big money like football and basketball.

But Simone earns millions of dollars from endorsing everything from **breakfast cereal** and **chocolate bars** to **sportswear** and **airlines** . . .

One of Simone's very best friends is her fellow gymnast **Jordan Chiles.** She has been in the **U.S. team** with Simone since 2013.

And Simone is one half of an American sporting superstar couple . . .

In 2023 she married her **NFL star boyfriend,** Chicago Bears safety **Jonathan Owens.**

Along with her huge haul of gymnastics medals, Simone's sporting achievements have won her a **string of awards** all over the world.

But the biggest of all came in 2022, when **President Joe Biden** presented Simone with the **Presidential Medal of Freedom.** The medal is the highest honor that can be given to an American civilian.

Simone is the *youngest* person ever to be awarded the medal.

Simone Biles is an **idol to millions** around the world—an American sports superstar and the **greatest gymnast of all time.**

Hers is a story of **strength, courage, overcoming adversity,** and a determination to succeed.

SIMONE BILES RULES!

QUIZ TIME!

How much do you know about SIMONE BILES? Try this quiz to find out, then test your friends!

1. Where was Simone born?

----

2. What was the name of the gymnastics club where Simone started?

----

3. Who was Simone's coach from 2005 to 2017?

----

4. Which is Simone's favorite gymnastics discipline?

----

5. In which year did Simone win her first World Championship medals?

----

6. What did the 2016 U.S. Olympics gymnastics team call themselves?

----

7. How many gold medals did Simone win at Rio 2016?

----

8. How many special skills are named after Simone?

----

9. What was the name of the condition Simone experienced during the 2020 Tokyo Olympics?

----

10. Which major honor was Simone awarded in 2022?

The answers are on the next page, *but no peeking!*

ANSWERS

1. Columbus, Ohio

2. Bannon's Gymnastix

3. Aimee Boorman

4. Floor exercise

5. 2013

6. The Final Five

7. Four

8. Five

9. The "twisties"

10. The Presidential Medal of Freedom

GYMNASTICS WORDS
YOU SHOULD KNOW

Skill
A single gymnastics move

Salto
The name for any type
of flip in the air

Layout
A salto (flip) in a
completely stretched-out
position

Olympics
The biggest international
mixed-sports event,
held every four years

**World Artistic
Gymnastics
Championships**
A huge international
gymnastics competition.
Held each year, except
in Olympic years

HAVE YOU READ ANY OF THESE OTHER BOOKS FROM THE SUPERSTARS SERIES?

SOCCER SUPERSTARS

1 FOOTBALL SUPERSTARS
RONALDO RULES
• FACTS • STORIES • STATS
SIMON MUGFORD • DAN GREEN

2 FOOTBALL SUPERSTARS
MESSI RULES
SIMON MUGFORD • DAN GREEN

3 FOOTBALL SUPERSTARS
KANE RULES
SIMON MUGFORD • DAN GREEN

4 FOOTBALL SUPERSTARS
MBAPPÉ RULES
• FACTS • STORIES • STATS
SIMON MUGFORD • DAN GREEN

5 FOOTBALL SUPERSTARS
STERLING RULES
• FACTS • STORIES • STATS
SIMON MUGFORD • DAN GREEN

6 FOOTBALL SUPERSTARS
HAZARD RULES
• FACTS • STORIES • STATS
SIMON MUGFORD • DAN GREEN

7 FOOTBALL SUPERSTARS
RASHFORD RULES
• FACTS • STORIES • STATS
SIMON MUGFORD • DAN GREEN

8 FOOTBALL SUPERSTARS
VAN DIJK RULES
• FACTS • STORIES • STATS
SIMON MUGFORD • DAN GREEN

9 FOOTBALL SUPERSTARS
SALAH RULES
• FACTS • STORIES • STATS
SIMON MUGFORD • DAN GREEN

10 FOOTBALL SUPERSTARS
NEYMAR RULES
• FACTS • STORIES • STATS
SIMON MUGFORD • DAN GREEN

11 FOOTBALL SUPERSTARS
AGÜERO RULES
• FACTS • STORIES • STATS
SIMON MUGFORD • DAN GREEN

12 FOOTBALL SUPERSTARS
POGBA RULES
• FACTS • STORIES • STATS
SIMON MUGFORD • DAN GREEN

13 FOOTBALL SUPERSTARS
DE BRUYNE RULES
• FACTS • STORIES • STATS
SIMON MUGFORD • DAN GREEN

14 FOOTBALL SUPERSTARS
MANÉ RULES
• FACTS • STORIES • STATS
SIMON MUGFORD • DAN GREEN

15 FOOTBALL SUPERSTARS
SOUTHGATE RULES
• FACTS • STORIES • STATS
SIMON MUGFORD • DAN GREEN

16 FOOTBALL SUPERSTARS
ZLATAN RULES
• FACTS • STORIES • STATS •
SIMON MUGFORD • DAN GREEN

17 FOOTBALL SUPERSTARS
HAALAND RULES
SIMON MUGFORD • DAN GREEN

18 FOOTBALL SUPERSTARS
MARTENS RULES
SIMON MUGFORD • DAN GREEN

19 FOOTBALL SUPERSTARS
BRONZE RULES
SIMON MUGFORD • DAN GREEN

20 FOOTBALL SUPERSTARS
LEWANDOWSKI RULES
• FACTS • STORIES • STATS •
SIMON MUGFORD • DAN GREEN

21 FOOTBALL SUPERSTARS
GREALISH RULES
• FACTS • STORIES • STATS •
SIMON MUGFORD • DAN GREEN

22 FOOTBALL SUPERSTARS
FOOTBALL RULES THE WORLD
INCREDIBLE STORIES FROM THE BIGGEST GAME ON THE PLANET
SIMON MUGFORD • DAN GREEN

23 FOOTBALL SUPERSTARS
ENGLAND RULE
• FACTS • STORIES • STATS •
SIMON MUGFORD • DAN GREEN

24 FOOTBALL SUPERSTARS
SAKA RULES
• FACTS • STORIES • STATS •
SIMON MUGFORD • DAN GREEN

25 FOOTBALL SUPERSTARS
LIONESSES RULE
• FACTS • STORIES • STATS •
SIMON MUGFORD • DAN GREEN

26 FOOTBALL SUPERSTARS
LIVERPOOL RULE
• FACTS • STORIES • STATS •
SIMON MUGFORD • DAN GREEN

FOOTBALL SUPERSTARS
FOOTBALL JOKES RULE
SIMON MUGFORD • DAN GREEN

FOOTBALL SUPERSTARS
FOOTBALL QUIZZES RULE
SIMON MUGFORD • DAN GREEN

FOOTBALL SUPERSTARS
FOOTBALL ACTIVITIES RULE
SIMON MUGFORD • DAN GREEN

SPORTS SUPERSTARS

1 SPORTS SUPERSTARS
HAMILTON RULES
• FACTS • STORIES • STATS •
SIMON MUGFORD • DAN GREEN

2 SPORTS SUPERSTARS
RADUCANU RULES
• FACTS • STORIES • STATS •
SIMON MUGFORD • DAN GREEN

3 SPORTS SUPERSTARS
VERSTAPPEN RULES
• FACTS • STORIES • STATS •
SIMON MUGFORD • DAN GREEN

4 SPORTS SUPERSTARS
SIMONE BILES RULES
• FACTS • STORIES • STATS •
SIMON MUGFORD • DAN GREEN

COLLECT THEM ALL!

ABOUT THE AUTHORS

Simon's first job was at the Science Museum, making paper airplanes and blowing bubbles big enough for your dad to stand in. Since then, he's written lots of books about everything from dinosaurs and rockets to BMX bikes, soccer, and motorsport. He lives in Kent, England, with his wife and daughter, a dog, and a cat.

Dan has drawn silly pictures since he could hold a crayon. Then he grew up and started making books about stuff like people's jobs, soccer, big machines, space, *Doctor Who*, and *Star Wars*. He lives in Suffolk, England, with his wife, son, daughter, and a dog that takes him for very long walks.